LEARN ICT

Emails and Multimedia Messages

Anne Rooney

QED Publishing

QED

First published in the UK in 2004 by
QED Publishing
A Quarto Group Company
226 City Road
London, EC1V 2TT

www.qed-publishing.co.uk

A Catalogue record for this book is available
from the British Library.

ISBN 1 84538 272 2

Written by Anne Rooney
Consultant Philip Stubbs
Designed by Jacqueline Palmer
Editor Anna Claybourne
Illustrator John Haslam
Photographer Ray Moller
Models supplied by Scallywags
Additional artwork by Luki Sumner-Rooney

Creative Director Louise Morley
Editorial Manager Jean Coppendale

Printed and bound in China

The words in **bold** are
explained in the Glossary
on page 31.

Contents

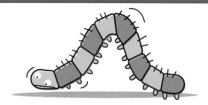

Do you use the computer to communicate with other people? You might send email, use a kids' chat or messaging service, look at web pages – or maybe make your own web pages or multimedia projects.

This time it's personal

When you send an email message, it's usually to someone you know, or at least someone whose name you know. It's a personal communication – something just between you and the other person. You can send the same email message to several people – to invite them to a party, for example – but it's still just between you and a few other people who you know.

Free-for-all

When you look at a web page, or even make your own, you're involved in a different kind of communication. You usually don't know the person who's made the web pages you look at. If you make your own web pages, you don't know the people who will look at them. Communications intended for lots of people are called **mass communications**.

In this book you'll find out about communicating with people you know, using email, and communicating with lots of people using web pages and multimedia.

Sending messages

Communicating with people using the computer is quite new. Before the 1990s, most people kept in touch by letter or phone. Mass communications were by radio, television, books and newspapers.

Early messages

Hundreds of years ago, there were no telephones, radios or televisions. To communicate over long distances, people had to use letters, or send messages using things like flags, smoke signals or drums.

In private

You couldn't have a very private conversation by smoke signal – lots of people could see it! Private communications in the past had to be sent by sealed letter. Sometimes they were even written in code, so that if anyone looked at the letter they couldn't see immediately what it said.

A message to keep

If you have a letter, you can keep it and look at it later. You can't do that with a phone call or a message sent by drums or flags. In the same way, you can keep an email, and you can print it if you want a copy to show other people or to put away.

Text messaging is another very new way of communicating instantly.

Top speed

Email is a very quick way of keeping in touch. Seconds after the message leaves your computer, it arrives at its destination, even if that's on the other side of the world. But to get a letter from Europe to China takes several days if it goes by plane, or weeks by sea.

Before you start any message, you should think about what you want to say and who you want to say it to. And think about whether using the computer is the best way – sometimes it might be better to phone or write a letter.

Multimedia

You've probably used CD-ROMs or websites that have a mixture of words, pictures, sounds and maybe even bits of movie. This is called multimedia. It's a great way of getting a message across, as you can use lots of different methods. If you wrote an essay on paper about, say, farm animals, you could use words and draw pictures. But on the computer you could make a multimedia page with the sounds the animals make and maybe even a video of them, too.

Click to:

See pig photos

Hear pig sounds

Watch the pig video!

All about pigs

The pigs kept on farms today are descended from wild boars.

Tell the world

If you make a multimedia show and put it on a web page, people all around the world can see it. The Web is the only way that you can quickly let anyone in the world see your work.

TAKE CARE

The Internet is used by lots of people, and some use it for things that aren't very nice. Make sure that a grown-up is with you while you are using the Web. Always check with a grown-up before reading email from someone you don't know, and never give your full name or address in an email message or on a web page. If you see something that upsets you, tell your teacher or parent.

To send an email, you need to know the email address of the person you're writing to – just as you need to know someone's house address to send them a letter.

Email addresses

An email address looks something like this:

myname@myemail.com

The first part says which person the email is for.

The '@' symbol is pronounced 'at'.

The last part is the computer address, called the domain.

 DO IT!

Once you've opened up your email program, look for an option called 'New message' or 'Create email'. Fill in the To and Subject fields, and make sure you've got the email address right. If it's not exactly correct, your message won't go to the right person. Click the 'Send' button when you've finished typing in your message.

Email addresses

You put the email address of the person you're writing to in the box marked 'To'.

What's it about?

There's a space for you to explain the subject of your email. This is what it's about – put something short and clear, like 'Party invitation' or 'Homework question'.

Often, people won't open an email if they don't know what it's about, especially if they don't know who it's from, so remember to fill this in.

To: flossie3@highgroveschool.com

Subject: My party

Hi Flossie -
I'm having a party next Saturday (14th) and I'd love you to come.
It will be at 2-5 pm at my house.
Bye!
Alice

Say something!

You don't have to be as formal in an email as a letter, but it's still polite to start with a greeting – maybe 'Dear George' or even 'Hi – how are you?' if it's someone you know well.

At the end of your message, don't forget to put a polite closing remark and your name.

So you know how to send a message, but what about how to receive one? If you send email messages to people, sooner or later someone will reply to you.

Getting a reply

You'll need to open your **mailbox** or **inbox** and then click on the new message to read it. There will be some way of telling the message is new. It might be shown in bold, or have a special picture next to it.

✉	**Re: My party**
✉	**Birthday present**
✉	**Hello from Jo**
✉	Cool site

A message you've read

A new message

Your computer might make a noise to let you know a new message has arrived.

Bling!

Hey! New messages

PRINT IT OUT

It can be useful to print out some of your email messages. You might want to use information in a message away from the computer, or let someone else use the computer. But don't print out all your email!

Your turn

Often, you need to send replies to email messages sent to you. Someone might ask you a question, or you may just be having a chat with them.

There will be a Reply button you can click. This starts a new email, with the right address filled in already. Usually, the other person's message is included, too. Type your own message and click on Send.

To:	frankieb@snailmail.com
Subject:	RE: my new story

Hi Frankie - good to hear from you
------Original Message-----
From: Frankie Baker [mail to:frankieb@snailmail.com]
Sent: 03 February 2004 10:25
To: Zeb
Subject: my new story

Hello Zeb
Do you remember you said you'd help me with my story?
Yes, of course I'll help - it will be fun.

This is my idea. Please let me know what you think. It is about a boy and his dog. They think a ghost lives in the shed in their garden

Have your say

Sometimes you might want to add comments, or make changes to what the original email says. If you put your comments in a different style, such as bold, that will help the person who sent you the message to see which are your bits.

The address book

Email addresses aren't always very easy to remember, but if you get them wrong, your message won't get through. To help you, the computer keeps an **address book** for you.

Keep a list

In the address book, you can keep the email addresses of everyone you want to send messages to. It lists email addresses beside names, as shown below.

Make sure you type the email address in carefully when you put it in the address book.

DO IT!

You might need to open your email address book before you can add a name. Look for an option to 'Add name' or 'Add contact'.

Add name ▼

Address Book

Name	Email address
Alex	alex@7delaneyxy.co.uk
Gemma	gemmatan@adxserve.com
Grandma	aclayden@goonline.com
Jody	jody@theclayhouse.co.uk
Stephen	stephen@abxserve.com
Tariq	tkabdul229@goonline.com

I must email Grandma

Sending a message

When you want to send a message to someone in your address book, you just need to choose their name from the list and the computer will fill in the address in the 'To' space for you.

Add name ▼

Address Book

Name	Email address
Alex	alex@7delaneyxy.co.uk
Gemma	gemmatan@adxserve.com
Grandma	
Jody	
Stephen	
Tariq	

From: leanne@bananamail.com

To: aclayden@goonline.com

Subject: Summer holidays

Hello Grandma
How are you? - We were wondering if we could come
and visit in the summer holidays?
Dad says we'll be able to come
anytime in August...

DO IT!

When you want to use an address, you may be able to click on the 'To' button to see the list, or you might have to open the address book first and pick the person you want to write to.

Attachments

Sometimes words aren't enough, and you need to send something else with your email message. You can add a picture, a document you've written or even a sound file.

Sending extras

An email message is usually just plain words. If you want to show someone some work you've done, or perhaps send them a picture you've made, you can send another computer file along with your message. This is called an **attachment** or enclosure.

It's a bit like putting something else in an envelope along with a letter – like a photo or a drawing, for example.

DO IT!

Look for a button with a picture of a paper clip, or an option to 'Attach File'. You'll need to show the computer where on the computer disk the file is that you want to send, then click on Attach or OK to use it.

	Attach file
From:	Caitlin@snailmail.com
To:	alexb@junioremail.com

Getting attachments

If someone else sends you an email message with an attachment, you'll need to save the attachment and then open it. You'll need the right kind of computer program to open the attachment – so if they've sent you a picture, you'll need an art program.

🖇 ✉ **Re: My party**

✉ **Birthday present**

✉ **Hello from Jo**

🖇 ✉ My fish picture

From: Caitlin@snailmail.com

To: alexb@junioremail.com

Subject: My seahorse picture

Hello Alex
Here is my picture for our fish project.
Love Caitlin

sea horse.bmp

Take care

When you get an email with an attachment, there's usually a picture of a paper clip beside the message. If you get an attachment you're not expecting, or from someone you don't know, ask a grown-up before you open it.

DO IT!

Look for an option to save the attachment. You'll have to tell the computer where to keep it.

17

Share the message

You can make your own multimedia project with a special program such as PowerPoint, or by making a web page. Sometimes you can even do it in a word-processing program.

On the Web

Building a multimedia web page, or putting a multimedia presentation on a website, is a good way to share something **online** that's more exciting than just words.

You won't find out here how to put your multimedia work on an online website – that's something your teacher can do for you when you've finished building it. But you could send it as an email attachment to your friends!

Using multimedia

If you've used multimedia CD-ROMs and websites before, you'll know how they work. As well as the words and pictures on the screen, there are buttons or linked words that you can click on to go to more information, or to play a sound or video. Whether it's a word, a button or a picture that's linked, it's called a **hotspot** or **hyperlink**. The whole system of linked pages is called **hypertext**.

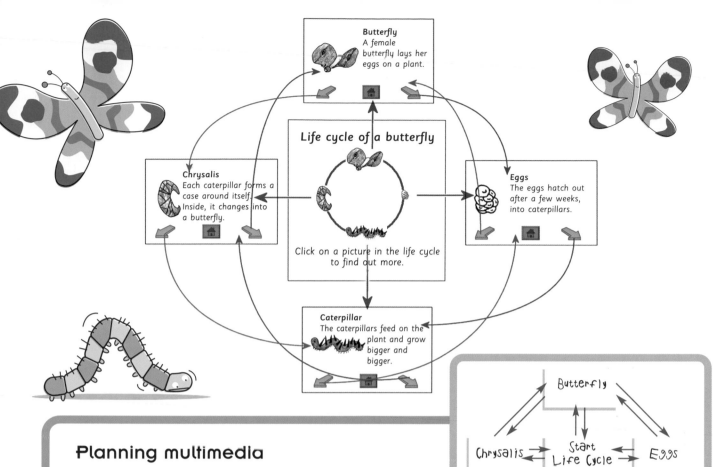

Butterfly
A female butterfly lays her eggs on a plant.

Life cycle of a butterfly

Click on a picture in the life cycle to find out more.

Chrysalis
Each caterpillar forms a case around itself. Inside, it changes into a butterfly.

Eggs
The eggs hatch out after a few weeks, into caterpillars.

Caterpillar
The caterpillars feed on the plant and grow bigger and bigger.

Planning multimedia

Work out what you're going to do before you start. You need to know where all your links will go, and make sure you have a sensible and clear structure.

It's a good idea to draw a flowchart to show where each link will go.

You'll need to work out how your pages are linked, which pictures and sounds to use and how to make sure people can get back to the start.

DO IT!

Find out how to create new pages in the multimedia program you're using. Look for an option like 'New page' or 'New file'.

You'll need to create each page, add the pictures and words, and then link them together.

Looking good

Take a look at some of the multimedia you use yourself and some of the web pages that you like. Try to see how the design of the pages helps you to understand and use a website or CD-ROM.

Design tips

In the best multimedia and web pages, you'll find:

The pages are consistent — they use the same types of headings, the same colours, and items that appear on more than one page are in the same place.

They have an area for any buttons that are used a lot, like a button to go back a page, or 'Contact' link.

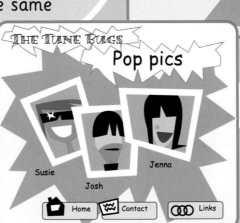

THE TUNE BUGS

3-piece pop band

- News
- Gigs
- MP3s
- Band bio
- Pop pics

Contact   Links

THE TUNE BUGS
Pop pics

Susie   Josh   Jenna

Home   Contact   Links

All the buttons are of a similar design.

If little pictures (icons) are used to show choices, it's obvious what they mean.

Your own designs

Sticking to a consistent design is important as it helps people feel at ease with your pages. They quickly learn how to use them and where to look.

Make sure the colours are suitable and the screen is easy to read. Headings should be big enough to stand out and pictures easy to see.

This is hard to read and the size of the words is confusing.

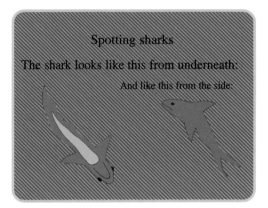

Spotting sharks

The shark looks like this from underneath:

And like this from the side:

This is much clearer.

Spotting sharks

The shark looks like this from underneath:

And like this from the side:

Who's it for?

Think about the people who will be using your presentation. You need to make sure both the design and the words suit your **audience**. So if you're making a multimedia guide to the school for new children in the reception class, it will have to be all pictures. But if you're presenting the results of your science investigation to your class, it can be more complicated.

DO IT!

Find out how to set the background colour for your pages, and how to change the style, colour and size of the words. You might be able to choose a pattern or picture for your background – but make sure the words will show up if you do this.

Make a sound

Most multimedia has some sound. You can record sounds, such as your own speech or singing – or you can make sounds using the computer.

Sound sequences

If you have a music program, you can build up a sound **sequence** on the computer that you can use in your multimedia show or web pages.

Usually, you need to click on a button to play a note or series of notes. Click on several buttons in turn to build up a musical sequence. Find out how to save your sequence so that you can use it in your multimedia work or web page.

When you put music in your multimedia, you should choose or make something suitable – don't use a sad piece of music in a page about parties or weddings!

Recording sound

Many computers have a microphone that you can use to record speech or other sounds. Speak clearly, or make your other sound clearly, and be careful to avoid background noise, such as other people talking, or chairs scraping on the floor.

Play back your sound and check it's all right. If not, record it again.

Extra sounds

You might be able to find sounds that you can use on the World Wide Web or a CD-ROM. For example, you could find animal noises, or sound effects such as wind or thunder. Ask for help from a grown-up if you're going to look on the Web for sounds.

Adding sound and pictures

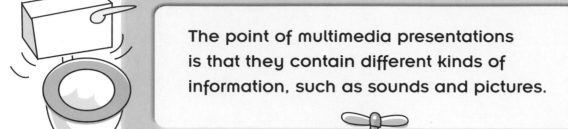

The point of multimedia presentations is that they contain different kinds of information, such as sounds and pictures.

DIY or ready-made?

Just as you can make your own sounds or get them from the Web or a CD-ROM, so you can draw your own pictures or use ready-made pictures. Make your own using an art program on the computer, or draw them on paper and scan them in with a **scanner**. Ready-made pictures are often called clip art. You can copy sounds and clip art from CD-ROMs or from the Web.

listen to the sound of thunder

Where do they go?

A picture can go straight onto your multimedia page. You'll need to link a sound to a button, picture or word so that people can play the sound when they want to by clicking on the link. Make sure it's clear what the button does. You might put a picture on the button, or put a label explaining what to do.

Types of file

When you want to add pictures and sounds to your multimedia pages, you'll need to make sure you save them as the right type of file, so find out what you need.

Check it!

Don't forget to check that your pages look good, have no mistakes and all the links work properly.

 # DO IT!

Look for an option to 'Import Picture' or 'Insert Picture'. You will have to tell the computer which picture file to use. You might need to move the picture, or change its size, once you've put it on the page. If you're using a multimedia program, you can change the size by dragging one of the 'handles' on the corners of the picture, or move the picture around the page by dragging it.

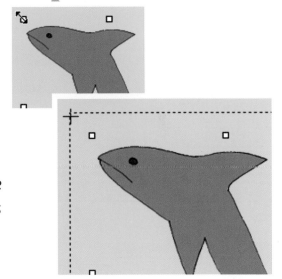

When you add a sound, you might have to choose a button, picture or word then add a sound to it, or add a link and choose your sound file as the linked file.

Finished!

When you've finished, save your work. If you're going to put it on a website, look for an option to 'Save as web page' or 'Save as HTML'. You'll need to keep all the pages and pictures together so that it all still works on the Web.

Projects to try

It's time to try it all out for yourself. These ideas should get you started, but of course you can change them to suit your own interests.

From: Caitlin@snailmail.com

To: helga@squekiemail.com

Subject: Questionnaire!

What colour socks are you wearing?

What's your favourite flavour crisps?

What's your favourite colour?

What's your favourite animal?

What are you scared of?

From: helga@squekiemail.com

To: Caitlin@snailmail.com

Subject: RE: Questionnaire!

Hi Caitlin

Here are my answers

What colour socks are you wearing?

Yellow and red stripes with blue spots

What's your favourite flavour crisps?

Ready salted

What's your favourite colour?

Green

Fun questionnaire

Make up a fun questionnaire that you can send to all your friends by email. Ask them to reply, filling in their answers to the questions. And then get them to do a questionnaire and send it to you so that you can have a go at replying!

Happy Birthday to you!

Make an **interactive** birthday card as a multimedia file or web page.

Either make your pictures on the computer, or draw them on paper and scan them in.

Make the page by adding the pictures and making sure they're in the right places and all the right sizes. Add the words you want — a suitable greeting in big, colourful letters.

Record yourself (or your friends, if you're shy) singing Happy Birthday. If you can't make a recording, see if you can put together a sound sequence instead.

Add a button to your card and attach the sound to it, so that when the button is clicked, the song or tune plays!

Story circle

Write a story with a group of friends using email. You'll need to agree some rules in advance – such as how much you can write each, and how many times the story will go around the group. The first person starts the story and emails it to the next person. That person adds more to the story and sends it on. Keep going until the story's finished.

If you've all got a word-processing program, you can write the story in that and send it as an attachment. Or why not make a picture instead? You can each add a bit of story and send it on.

When Tim woke up, he was sure something special was happening that day. Then he remembered! They were going to the Science Museum for Jessie's birthday...

The machine shook and shuddered and spun around, they saw wonderful colours – suddenly the machine stopped and landed with a thud...

The notice said: 'Heironymus Hill's Time Machine'. It was invented and built in 1759, but it had never worked...Tim and Jessie climbed into its large red seats...

Tim turned all six dials to the positions the notice described. At first, nothing happened. Then, slowly, the time machine began to tremble...

Form a pop band!

Make up a fantasy pop band with your friends and build a multimedia presentation about yourselves. You'll need to draw pictures of yourselves, or use photos you've scanned in or taken with a **digital camera**. Put a picture of an instrument by each person. Find **sound samples** for each instrument and add those to your page. And then add a page about each member of the band – make up your fantasy biogs and link them in!

Our Band

Rajal plays guitar

Luki plays drums

Communicate Online and the National Curriculum

This book will help a child to cover work units 3B, 3E and 6A of the National Curriculum for England and Wales.

The National Curriculum for ICT stresses that ICT should be integrated with other areas of study. This means that a child's use of ICT should fit naturally into other areas of the curriculum. It can be achieved by tasks such as:

• Gathering information for a report or project by emailing people and asking them questions.

• Creating a multimedia presentation using PowerPoint or as a web page to explain a process, such as the water cycle.

• Exchanging email drafts of stories with a friend as attachments, adding annotations to the email or the attached story and sending it back.

• Producing a multimedia page about musical instruments with sound samples from the instruments described.

Children should incorporate planning, drafting, checking and reviewing their work in all projects. They should discuss with others how their work could be improved, whether ICT methods are the best choice for a given task and how ICT methods compare with manual methods. They should look at ways of combining ICT and manual methods of working.

National Curriculum resources online

ICT programme of study at Key Stage 2 in the National Curriculum:

www.nc.uk.net

On teaching ICT in other subject areas:

www.ncaction.org.uk/subjects/ict/inother.htm

ICT schemes of work (you can download a printable copy):

www.standards.dfes.gov.uk/schemes2/it/

The schemes of work for Key Stage 2 suggest ways that ICT can be taught in years 3–6.

Further resources

It's important to make sure that children use the World Wide Web safely. The following sites give advice on how you can protect your children when they work online and how to help them to use the Web sensibly.

www.safekids.com

www.thinkuknow.co.uk

www.yahooligans.com/parents/

www.getnetwise.org

www.nchafc.org.uk/itok/

Glossary

Address book

List of email addresses kept on your computer.

Attachment

Extra file sent with an email message.

Audience

The people who will see your multimedia presentation.

Digital camera

Camera that stores pictures in a computer memory chip rather than on a film.

Hotspot

Part of a page you can click on to follow a link.

Hyperlink

Word or picture linked to another page.

Hypertext

System of interlinked pages of words and pictures.

Inbox

Place where email messages are stored when they arrive on your computer.

Interactive

Able to respond to users actions or choices by, for example, playing a sound or displaying another page.

Mailbox

Place where email messages are stored when they arrive on your computer.

Mass communication

A message intended for lots of people at once.

Online

Connected to the Internet, or on the World Wide Web.

Scanner

Device for copying pictures from paper into the computer.

Sequence

Series of items, such as musical sounds or notes.

Sound sample

Short recording of sound, such as speech, music or sound effects.

Index